Build Your Comput

Building your computer is not difficult…There's a rush that you get when you press the power button for the first time on a new computer. The quiet blow of the fans, the reassuring beeps, and the glow of a monitor all signal the completion of another successful build. That feeling of unknown and anticipation is one of the driving forces for computer enthusiasts, and building your own computer is the perfect entry point. Everything from a simple office PC, to media centers, to high-end gaming rigs are all cheaper and more exciting to build for yourself. Follow this guide to learn how.

Part 1 of 8: Gathering Your Components

1

Determine the function of the computer. If you're building a computer to use in the home office for word processing and emails, you'll have much different requirements than if you're building a computer for high-end gaming. The role of your computer will heavily dictate the components that you will need.

o   Don't waste money on expensive parts you may not need. If your PC will be performing only basic functions, you can save money by getting less powerful but more affordable components. Also you can save money by buying second hand products off ebay. Be careful buying used parts! Make sure they have been tested and work

2. 2

Find the parts you need. Regardless of the final function of your computer, every computer needs the same basic components:

- **Processor** – This is the brain of your computer. Almost all processors are multi-core, meaning they are essentially multiple processors in one. Compare specs and find a processor that has the speed that you will need to run the programs you want. Also take into account power usage and ease of cooling.
  - If you want performance, go with Intel. AMD is cheaper, but they are not as fast.
- **Motherboard** – The motherboard is what connects all of the internal components of your computer. The processor you purchase will determine the type of motherboard you will need. Different processors have different "socket" sizes, and only work with motherboards that support that socket.
  - Motherboards come in many form-factors, but the most common are ATX and MicroATX. ATX is the standard full-size motherboard. If you are building a typical tower computer, look for ATX motherboards. µATX boards are smaller than the standard ATX board, and are better if you want a smaller case and have no need for more than four expansion slots.
  - Make sure that your motherboard supports all of the other components that you wish to install. If you are planning on installing a high-end graphics card, the motherboard will need to support the PCI Express interface. If you want to install lots of RAM, your motherboard will need to be able to hold at least 4 sticks.
  - Your choice here will depend on what processor you have, how much memory you want, the size of your case, and how many drives you want to connect to it.
- **RAM** – RAM (Random Access Memory) is where programs store information that they are using. If you don't have enough RAM, your programs will run much slower than they should. The RAM you can purchase is dictated by the motherboard that you choose. The speed of the RAM that you install must be supported by the motherboard.[1]
  - RAM should always be installed in matching pairs of sticks. All the RAM in the system should be the same speed, and preferably the same make and model. For example, if you want 8 GB of RAM, you can install two matching 4 GB sticks or four matching 2 GB sticks.
  - If you intend to use more than 4 GB of RAM, you will need to install a 64-bit operating system. 32-bit operating systems do not recognize more than 4 GB of RAM, even if more is installed.
- **Hard drive** – Your hard drive stores all of your data and installed programs. Storage space has gotten much cheaper over the years, and it is easy to find up to a couple of terabytes of storage for just a little money.
  - Hard drives come in many speeds, the most common being 7200 RPM, 10,000 RPM, or Solid State. Solid state drives are the fastest available, but the cost is significantly higher than a traditional drive.

- Regular old mechanical hard disk drives are cheap right now, but solid state drive prices are dropping like crazy. If you want fast and reliable, go with solid state.
- Putting your operating system and critical programs on a smaller drive, and then storing everything else on a larger drive, will lead to faster loading times for your system.

- **Video card** – A dedicated graphics card is essential for playing the latest games, but not a major issue for an office computer. Intel motherboards have integrated graphics, so you don't need a dedicated card if you're planning to use the computer for web browsing and emails, but some AMD 'boards will need a video card.
- **Case** – This is what houses your computer components. The size of the case will be determined by how many drives you will be installing, as well as the size of your motherboard. Cases range from cheap and functional to flashy and expensive.[2]
  - If you intend to run a lot of high-end components, you will be dealing with a lot more heat output than slower components. Choose a case that promotes good airflow and allows you to install more fans.
- **Power supply** - The power supply powers all of your components in your computer. Some cases come with a power supply already installed, but most require you to provide your own. The power supply should be powerful enough to charge all of your components, but not so powerful that you waste electricity by powering more than you need.

Research every component you intend to purchase. Read magazines and online consumer review sites for more information. Online forums like AnandTech are also very helpful when specific information is needed. Remember, this is one of the most important steps, because everything will depend on your hardware. There are many guides and reviews available from online magazines and consumer review websites. Samples include:

- *PC World*
- *PC Magazine*
- *Maximum PC*
- *Custom PC*

Part 2 of 8: Getting Started

1

Open the case. You might want to wear gloves or some sort of hand protection, as the inside of the case does not have ground down metal and could be very sharp in some cases.

2

Install the power supply. Some cases come with the power supply already installed, while others will require you to purchase the power supply separately and install it yourself. Make sure that the power supply is installed in the correct orientation, and that nothing is blocking the power supply's fan.

- o   Make sure that your power supply is powerful enough to handle all of your components. This is especially important in high-end gaming computers, as dedicated graphics cards can draw a significant amount of power.

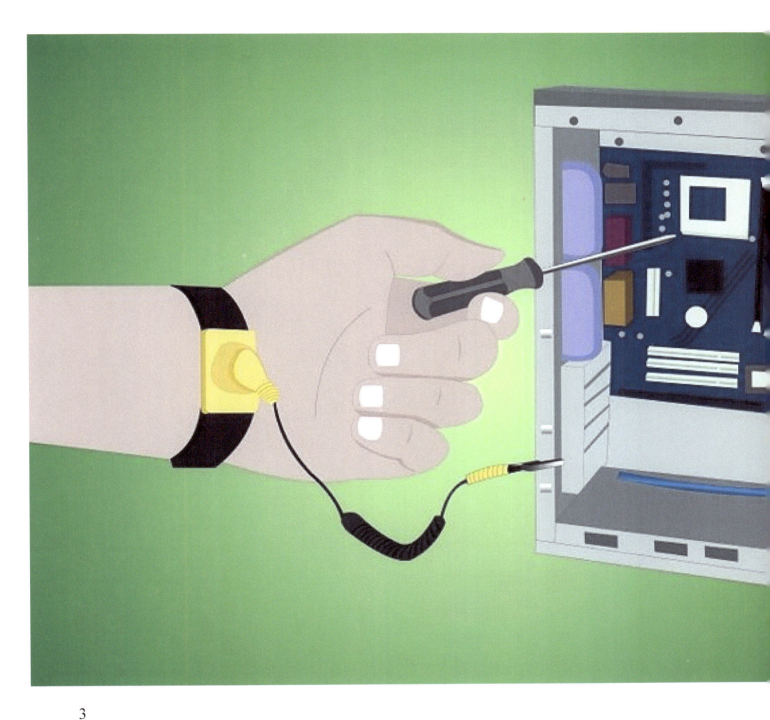

3

Ground yourself. Use an antistatic wrist-strap cable to prevent Electrostatic Discharge (ESD) which can be deadly to computer electronics. If you can't get an antistatic wrist-strap cable, plug your grounded power supply unit to an outlet (but don't turn it on), and keep your hand on the grounded unit whenever you touch any ESD-sensitive items.

Part 3 of 8: Installing the Motherboard

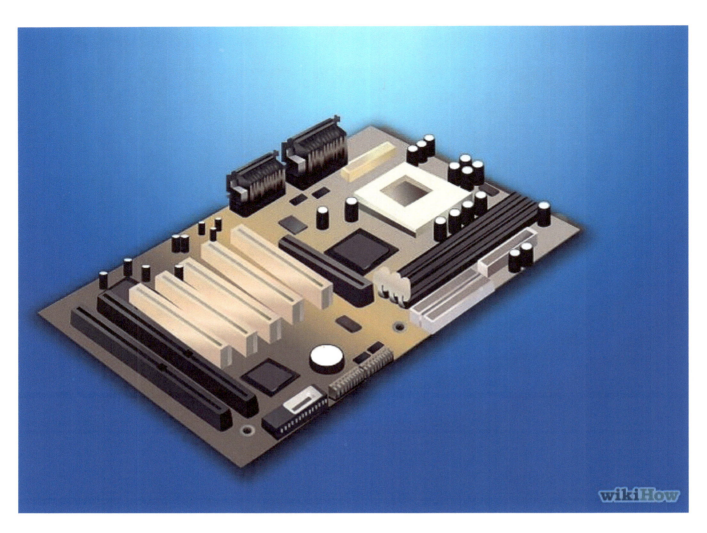

1

Remove the motherboard from its packaging. Place it on top of its box. DO NOT place it on top of the anti-static bag as the outside is conductive. You will be adding components to the motherboard before installing it in the case, as it is easier to access the motherboard before installing it.

2

Remove the processor from its packaging. Observe the missing pins in the processor and match these with the socket on the motherboard. On many processors there will be a little gold arrow in the corner that you can use to orient the processor properly.

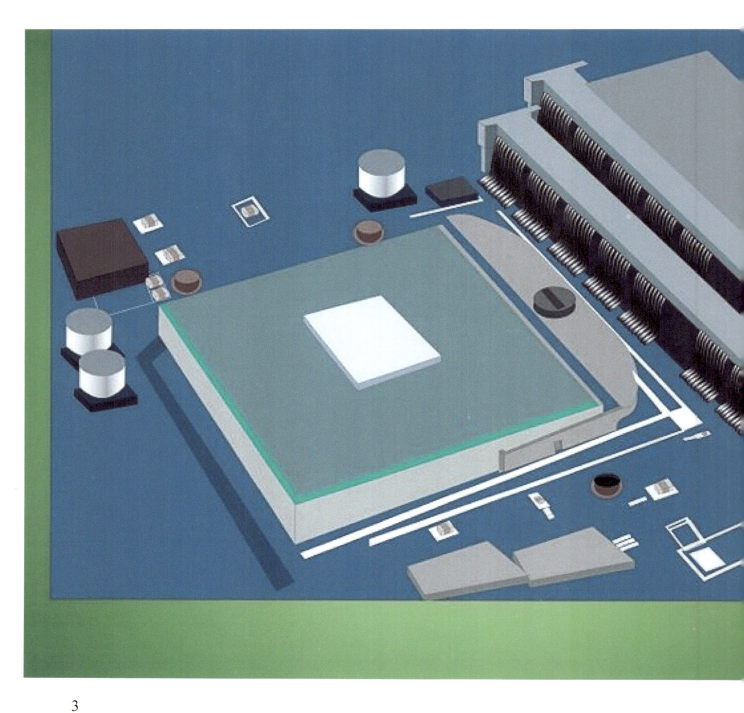

3

Insert the processor in the motherboard. Open the CPU socket and carefully insert the processor (no force needed). If it doesn't slip right in, or it feels like you have to push, it is probably misaligned. Close the socket and ensure the CPU is secure. Some sockets have small arms while others have complex assemblies to open and close the socket.[3]

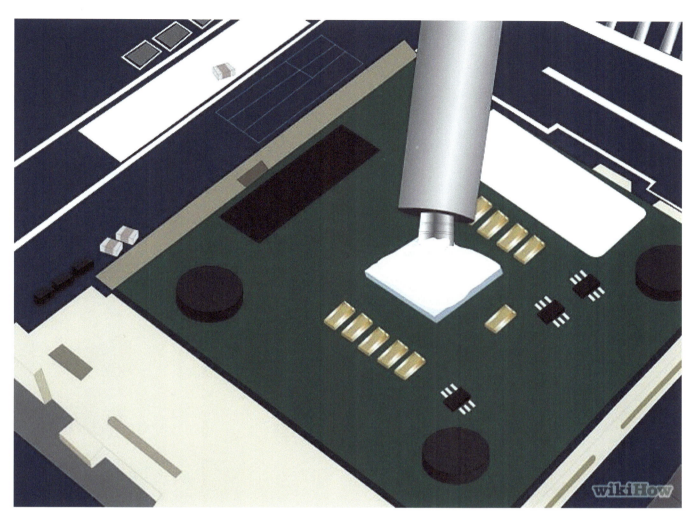

4

Apply good thermal paste to the CPU. Put only a dot of thermal paste on the CPU. Adding too much thermal paste will slow the transfer of heat, making it more difficult to cool the CPU quickly.

- o Some processors that come with heatsinks do not need thermal paste because the heat sink already has thermal paste applied by the factory. Check the bottom of the heatsink unit before applying paste to the processor.[4]

5

Attach the heat sink. This varies from heat sink to heat sink, so read the instructions. Most stock coolers attach directly over the processor and clip into the motherboard. Aftermarket heatsinks may have brackets that need to be attached underneath the motherboard. Refer to your heatsink's documentation for exact instructions.

2. 6

Install the RAM. Place the RAM in the proper slots by opening the latches and pushing the RAM in until the little handles can lock it into position. Note how the RAM and slots are keyed--line them up so they will fit in properly. When pushing, press both sides of the RAM module with equal force. If RAM sockets have two colors, this may indicate the priority slots in case if you are not using all available slots.

- o Make sure that you install the RAM in the appropriate matching slots. Check your motherboard's documentation to ensure that you are installing the RAM in the correct location.

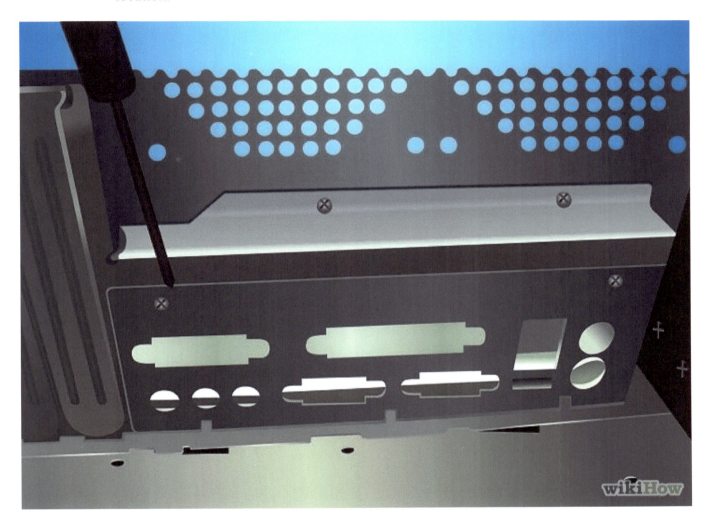

7

Install the I/O backplate on the back of your case. Many modern cases do not have a pre installed backplate, but your motherboard should come with its own backplate. Some older cases have pre-instlalled I/O back plates, but it is unlikely that the case will have an appropriate backplate for your motherboard.

- o Removing the existing backplate may take a bit of force. Sometimes they have screws to hold them in place, but most are held in only by friction. Pop it out by pressing on the bracket from the rear side of the case.

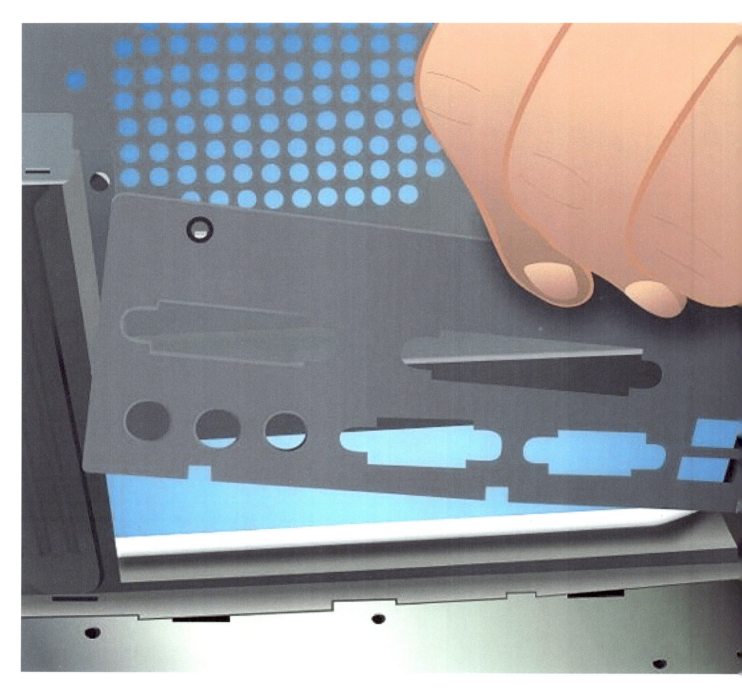

8

Knock out any tabs covering I/O components up on the motherboard's backplate. Push the new backplate into place in the back of the case. Make sure to install it the correct direction.[5]

3. 9

Install the standoffs in the correct positions. Almost all cases come with a little baggie that has standoffs in it. Standoffs raise the motherboard off of the case, and allow screws to be inserted into them.

o   Your case most likely has more holes available than your motherboard supports. The number of spacers required will be determined by the number of shielded holes in the motherboard. Position the motherboard to discover where to screw in the standoffs.

10

Secure the motherboard. Once the standoffs are installed, place the motherboard in the case and push it up against the I/O backplate. All of the back ports should fit into the holes in the I/O backplate. Use the screws provided to secure the motherboard to the standoffs through the shielded screw holes on the motherboard.

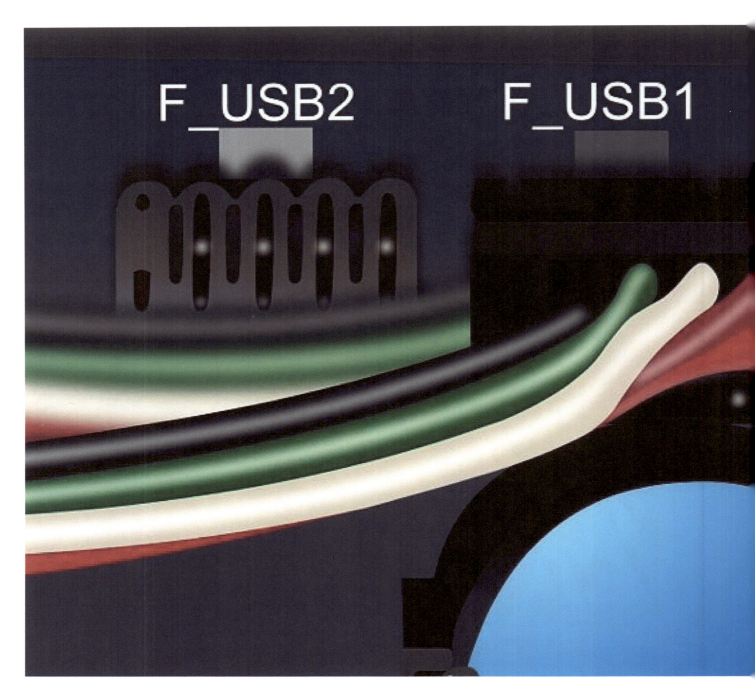

Plug in the case connectors. These tend to be located together on the motherboard near the front of the case. The order in which these are connected will depend on which is easiest. Make sure that you connect the USB ports, the Power and Reset switches, the LED power and hard drive lights, and the audio cable (HDAudio or AC97). Your motherboard's documentation will show you where on your motherboard these connectors attach.

- There is typically only one way that these connectors can attach to the motherboard. Don't try to force anything to fit.

Part 4 of 8: Installing a Graphics Card

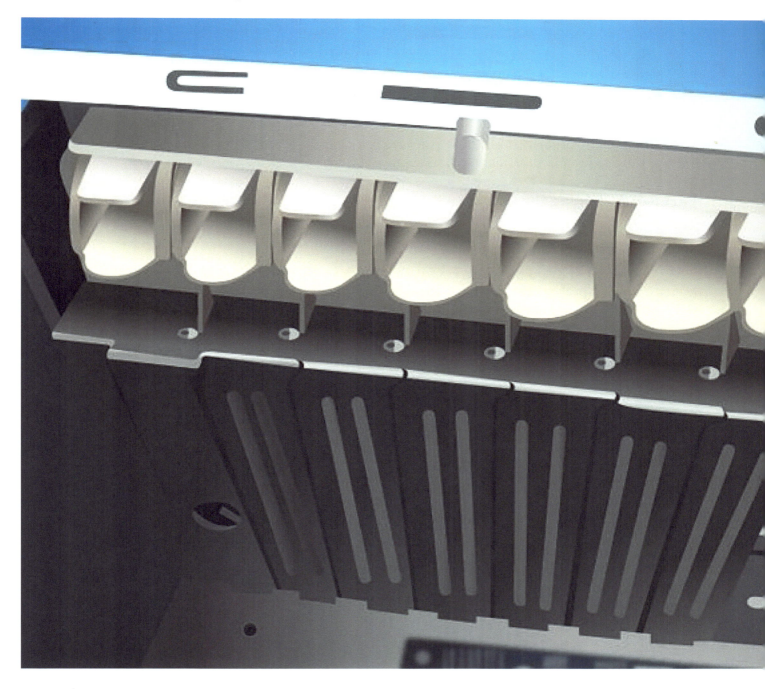

1

Remove the back panel covers that line up with the PCI-E slot. Almost all modern graphics cards use PCI-E. Some will require you to remove two of the protective plates as opposed to just one. You may have to punch the plates out of the case.

1. 2

Insert the graphics card. You may have to bend a tab on the slot to allow the graphics card to be inserted. The tab will help lock the graphics card in place (this is more important for bulkier, high-end cards). Apply light, even force until the card is seated uniformly, and the back panel lines up.

2. 3

Secure the card. Once you have inserted the card, use a screw to secure it to the back panel of the case. If you don't secure your card, you could end up damaging it in the long run.

3. 4

Install any other PCI cards. If you have any other PCI cards that you are going to add, such as a dedicated sound card, the installation process is the same as the video card process.

Part 5 of 8: Adding the Drives

1. 1

Remove any front panel covers for the drives you are inserting. Most cases have panels in the front that protect the drive bays. Remove the panels for the locations that you want to install you optical drives. You do not need to remove any panels for hard drives.

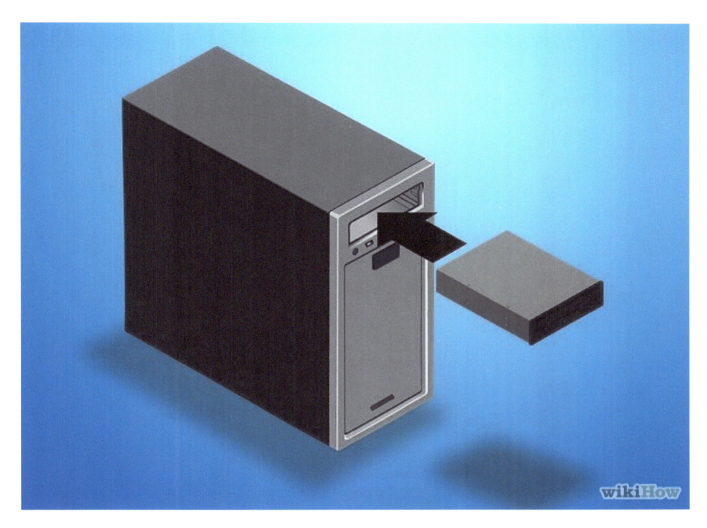

2

Insert the optical drives in from the front of the case. Almost all cases have cages built in that allow the drive to rest and fit snugly. Once the drive is lined up with the front panel of the computer, secure it with screws on each side of the drive.

2. 3

Install the hard disk. Slide the hard drive into the appropriate 3.5" bay in the inside of the case. Some cases have removable brackets that you can install on the hard drive first before sliding it in. Once the drive has been inserted into the cage, secure it on both sides with screws.

3. 4

Connect the SATA cables. All modern drives use SATA cables to connect the drive to the motherboard. Connect the cable to the SATA port on the drive, and then connect the other end to a SATA port on the motherboard. Hard drives use the same cables as optical drives.[6]

- o   For easier troubleshooting, connect your hard drive to the first SATA port on the motherboard, and then connect your other drives to subsequent SATA ports. Avoid plugging your drives into random SATA ports.

- SATA cables have the same connector on both sides. You can install the cable in either direction.

Part 6 of 8: Wiring the Computer

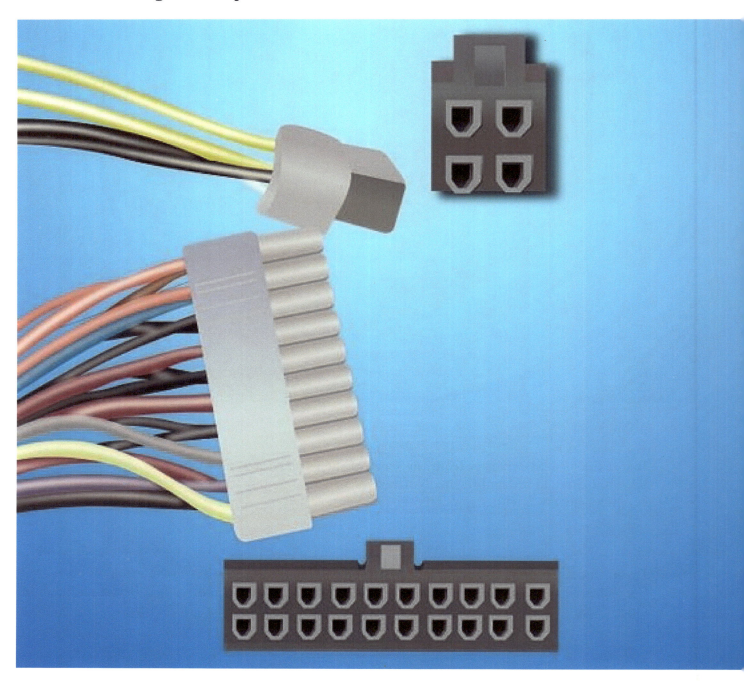

1

Connect the power supply to the motherboard. Most modern motherboards have a 24-pin connector and a 6- or 8-pin connector. Both of these need to be connected for your motherboard to function. Power supply cables only fit into the slots that they are designed for. Push the connectors all the way in until the latch clicks.

- o   The 24-pin connector is the largest connector on the power supply.

2. 2

   Connect the power supply to the video card. If you have a dedicated video card, chances are it needs to be powered as well. Some require one connector, while others require two. The port is usually on the top of the video card.

3. 3

   Connect the power supply to the drives. All of your drives need to be connected to the power supply using SATA power connectors. These power connectors are the same for optical and hard drives.

4. 4

   Adjust your wire placement. One of the keys to good airflow is placing your wires out of the way. Trying to effectively wire the inside of the case can be a frustrating experience, especially if you are building a smaller tower. Use zip ties to bundle cables together and place them in unused drive bays. Make sure that the cables will not get in the way of any fans.

Part 7 of 8: Installing More Fans

1. 1

   Connect your case fans. Almost all cases come installed with one or two fans. These fans need to be attached to the motherboard in order to function.

2

Install new fans. If you are running lots of high-end components, you will likely need extra cooling. 120mm fans are typically fairly quiet and significantly increase airflow through your computer.

2. 3

Optimize your fan setup. Front and top fans should be sucking air in, while side and rear fans should be pushing air out. This keeps a good flow of fresh, cool air moving over your motherboard. You can see which direction the fan will blow by inspecting the top of the fan housing. Almost all fans have small arrows printed which shows which direction they blow.

Part 8 of 8: Booting it Up

1. 1

Put the case back together. It is highly recommended that you don't run your computer with the case open. Cases are designed to maximize air flow, and when a case is open the airflow is not as effective. Make sure that everything is screwed close. Most cases use thumbscrews so that you don't need tools to open and close the case.

2. 2

   Plug in your computer. Attach a monitor to the computer, either through the graphics card or through a port on the back of the motherboard plate. Attach a keyboard and mouse to the USB ports in either the front or back of the computer.

   o   Avoid plugging in any other devices until after you have finished setting up the operating system.

3. 3

   Power on your computer. You won't be able to do much since you don't have an operating system installed, but you can check to see that all of your fans are working and that the computer completes its POST (Power On Self Test) successfully.

4. 4

   Run MemTest86+. This program is available to download for free and can be booted from a CD or USB drive without an operating system installed. This will let you test your memory sticks before you proceed to install the operating system. Memory sticks have a higher rate of failure than most computer components, especially if they are budget-priced, so it is wise to test them first.

   o   You may have to set your computer to boot from CD or USB first, instead of booting from the hard drive. Enter your BIOS settings when you first start the computer, and then navigate to the Boot menu. Select the appropriate drive that you want to boot from.

5. 5

   Install your operating system. Home-built computers can install either Microsoft Windows or a Linux distribution. Windows costs money, but benefits from having compatibility with nearly every program and piece of hardware. Linux is free and supported by a community of developers, but cannot run many programs designed for Windows. Some proprietary hardware does not work properly either.

6. 6

   Install your drivers. Once your operating system is installed, you will need to install your drivers. Almost all of the hardware that you purchased should come with discs that contain the driver software needed for the hardware to work. Modern versions of Windows and Linux will install most drivers automatically when connected to the internet.